THE MOMMY-DADDY FACTOR
Blending Your Family God's Way

By:
Dr. Rhonda S. Sullivan

MOMMY-DADDY FACTOR:
Blending Your Family God's Way

Printed in the United States of America
©2007 by Dr. Rhonda S. Sullivan
Publisher: We Family Ministries
P.O. Box 8812
Jacksonville, FL 32239
wefamily904@aol.com

Library of Congress Cataloging
ISBN-13: 978-0978854515
ISBN-10: 0978854519

INTRODUCTION

The divorce rate in the U.S. for first marriages is about 50% and 60% for second marriages. About 20% of U.S kids live in stepfamilies. Another 20% are shuffled between two parents.[1] This is the sad reality that the world wants you to accept. But these statistics do not have to be a reality for your life and the life of your family. God's word offers promise. Through obedience to his word you will have peace, joy, love, hope, and success in every good work. Don't accept the world's standards for your life.

I am writing this book from both sides of the fence. In my first marriage, I chose a mate and married him only to find that he had numerous problems. I tried to fix the many problems in my marriage on my own; the world's way. I combated his drug addiction with anger, deception, and strife. I countered his verbal and physical abuse with rebellion and unforgiveness. That marriage ended after four years. To my surprise, divorce catapulted my daughter into a deep depression. It was a long painful struggle back to wholeness for both her and I. In 2006, I married my soul mate. "Soul" referring to an amazing man of God and the one that I believe God had for me all along. We have two beautiful daughters. We blended our

---

[1] National Center for Health Statistics. (2004) Births, Marriages, Divorces, and Deaths: Provisional Data for November 2003. National Vital Statistics Report, 52(20), Table A. Retrieved 9/7/2006.

family God's way and live under the instruction of the Holy Spirit. By doing so, we have been able to avoid many of the struggles that many blended families face. I am blessed to be able to say that we are no longer a blended family but one unit. We serve together, love together, and live together.

My experience serves as undeniable evidence that God's way is the only way. As you read, search yourself to identify your strengths and weaknesses. Seek God for insight into his path for your life and the lives of your family members. Pray for guidance and protection during the process of blending your family. As the enemy comes to bring division, FIGHT! Fight for your life and the life of your family. This book will equip you for the battle.

TABLE OF CONTENTS

PRIORITY ONE

Keeping Your Marriage First

When Jesus had finished saying these things, he left Galilee and went into the region of Judea to the other side of the Jordan. Large crowds followed him, and he healed them there. Some Pharisees came to him to test him. They asked, "Is it lawful for a man to divorce his wife for any and every reason?" "Haven't you read," he replied, "that at the beginning the Creator 'made them male and female,' and said, 'For this reason a man will leave his father and mother and be united to his wife, and the two will become one flesh'? So they are no longer two, but one. Therefore what God has joined together, let man not separate."

Matthew 19:1-6

Your Family God's Way

Marriage is a covenant between a man and a woman. It is holy and sanctified by God. God ordains marriage to be the prerequisite to building any family. The passage above demonstrates the importance of this holy covenant. It reveals the importance of becoming one-flesh. This one-flesh union takes priority as it is the facilitator of everything else in the family structure, children, prosperity, and growth.

Take time to nurture your marriage by spending quality time alone. Keep your line of communication open. Open communication allows you to resolve areas of conflict in your relationship. Setting aside "talk time" is a great way to remain unified in thought and action. During "talk time", anything goes. Don't focus on any specific topic. Just let the conversation flow. Speak freely about the "ups" and "downs" and anything else that comes to mind. God knows what you and your spouse need, not just physically but spiritually and emotionally, as well. Allow the Holy Spirit to guide your conversation. He will supply all of your needs.

Spouses need to know that their efforts are not in vain. They need to be appreciated and to know that they are loved, especially as they give love to others. I am employed outside the home. My husband works from home. He keeps our house spotless, takes our girls to school and picks them up, helps with homework, washes clothes and dishes; and the list goes on. I never take for granted that the things that he does for our family are in agreement with God's word. They are truly a blessing to me and our children. I express my thankfulness in numerous ways. One major way is that I tell him how much I appreciate all that he does, even the minor things. I tell him daily how amazing he is as a husband, a father, and as a man. If you are in a situation where your negatives far outweigh the positives, pray for your spouse's deliverance from whatever is hindering their ability to be all that God has called them to be. Activate your faith. Believe for spiritual growth and the insight to recognize the negatives as sin that needs to be removed. Praise God for what you know is yours. God said that joy, peace, and prosperity are yours and it is if you have the faith to claim it.

Sexual intimacy is equally as important. 1 Corinthians 7:5 says that *the two must not deprive one another except by mutual consent and for a time, so that you may devote yourselves to prayer. Then come together again so that Satan will not tempt you because of your lack of self-control.* This scripture stresses the ability of Satan to gain access to your family in the presence of unmet intimacy needs. Experts refer to the resulting arguments and strife as "sexual frustration". Unmet sexual needs as well as any other unmet need will lead to sin. You or your spouses may look for fulfillment outside the marriage bed in situations where emotional and physical needs go unmet. This can lead to destruction of the marriage or the entire family unit.

Blended families bring varied backgrounds encompassing a multitude of morals, values, and beliefs. This may be a source of tension and strife within the new family. But this is not God's plan. As the trials come, remember your ability to impact your family through your unity, love, and respect. You are the model in which your children will imitate. Whether the example you set is good or bad is up to you. Contentious parents breed unruly children. Fulfilled, stable, and happy parents raise children with the same traits.
Making the preservation of your marriage priority is essential to the preservation of Godly families. A husband is to love his wife as himself and the wife

must respect her husband as she does the Lord. (Ephesians 5:33) As the two walk in obedience to these commands, contention, strife, isolation, and any other sinful emotion cannot exist. By keeping this principle of obedience in the forefront of thoughts and actions, a blended family can overcome anything.

Recognize the positive. Acknowledge all of the good things that your mate does. God's word provides a template for the roles of husbands and wives. This determines what is good or bad. Husbands should be considerate to their wives and treat them with respect. The man must remain the head of the household. He must earn the respect of his spouse and his children. The wife is to respect and submit to her husband as unto the Lord. This includes the importance of respecting the parenting style of the each parent and the necessity of resolving conflict amiably. Marriage is a life-long process. Success takes continuously working at it. Foster love and admiration. If you do not love each other, when the kids leave, you will be lost. The greatest thing you can do for your children is to love your spouse.

The Mirror
What distractions need to be removed to make my marriage a priority?

Five Second Fix-it:
Lord, I will honor marriage as a testament to the love I have for you. Thank you for helping me to keep my marriage a priority and for removing the distractions

that seek to hinder our growth as individuals and as a holy union.
Hebrews 13:4

YOUR TRIAL...HIS BATTLE

Seek God

Jesus entered Jericho and was passing through. A man was there by the name of Zacchaeus; he was a chief tax collector and was wealthy. He wanted to see who Jesus was, but being a short man he could not, because of the crowd. So he ran ahead and climbed a sycamore-fig tree to see him, since Jesus was coming that way. When Jesus reached the spot, he looked up and said to him, "Zacchaeus, come down immediately. I must stay at your house today." So he came down at once and welcomed him gladly. All the people saw this and began to mutter, "He has gone to be the guest of a 'sinner.'" But Zacchaeus stood up and said to the Lord, "Look, Lord! Here and now I give half of my possessions to the poor, and if I have cheated anybody out of anything, I will pay back four times the amount." Jesus said to him, "Today salvation has come to this house, because this man, too, is a son of Abraham. For the Son of Man came to seek and to save what was lost."

Luke 19:1-10

Your Family God's Way

Zacchaeus, a sinner, desperately wanted to see Jesus. He did not let his short stature hinder him. He sought Jesus from the heights of that sycamore tree. As he reached out to Jesus and repented of his sin he was rewarded for his efforts. He was welcomed into the presence of God, the origin of all good things.

As your family is being blended you will face many trials. No matter what you encounter, remember to seek God for whatever you need. Seek him and he will be found. (1 Chronicles 28:9) He will hear your cries, answer your prayers, and reward your diligence. Separate the sin from the sinner. Although sin must be confronted and rebuked, do not forget that you are obligated to help those trapped in sin to return to righteousness. Do not make excuses for what you believe may be a bad situation. Look for opportunities to be an Godly example to the people around you instead of finding faults in their behavior. Pray to, praise, and believe God in faith for the loving, God-led family that you will have. It is yours because God's word says it is.

The Mirror
In what areas of my life have I not sought God for the help I need?

Five Second Fix-it:
Thank you God, for allowing your grace to cover me through my trial and so that I will have everything that I need. Thank you for helping me to abound in every good work.
2 Corinthians 9:8

THE SACRIFICE

Love

"You have heard that it was said, 'Love your neighbor and hate your enemy.' But I tell you: Love your enemies and pray for those who persecute you, that you may be sons of your Father in heaven. He causes his sun to rise on the evil and the good, and sends rain on the righteous and the unrighteous. If you love those who love you, what reward will you get? Are not even the tax collectors doing that? And if you greet only your brothers, what are you doing more than others? Do not even pagans do that? Be perfect, therefore, as your heavenly Father is perfect.
Matthew 5:43-48

Your Family God's Way

It is easy to love those who love you. But, what about the ones who are not so nice to you? What about those around you who do not love you the way you think you should be loved? Aren't you commanded to love them as well? According to the scripture above, you are not only commanded to love them but to pray for them as well. This does not just apply to people on your job, the rude cashier at the local grocery, or the person who cuts you off on the freeway. It is an especially important command for those people God entrusts to you, your step-children.

Children of blended families experience many different emotions. Among them are anger, sadness, and disappointment. You may become the target of their anger even if you don't deserve it. You may be isolated by their need to find comfort in their own isolation. Their feelings of disappointment may manifest as distrust and frustration. All of these emotions can push you away, but only if you allow them to.

God's word requires that you abound in love, remain slow to anger, and forgive. Obeying these commands will save many blended families from destruction. Be an imitator of God. (Ephesians 5:1) Living a Christ-like life counters Satan's attacks and prevents you from falling into sin, even as a response to hurt and pain. You must do more than what comes naturally to you. Loving your spouse or your biological children is easy. It is expected. But loving children who may not be so loving towards you is the real test of your love for God. Can you obey his Word even in the face of pain and disappointment? Can you love even when love hurts?

Preserving your family demands that you honor God above your own feelings. Obedience to God's word provides the strength to endure the trials of life, even an unruly or distant step-child. This does not mean agreeing with or accepting their negative behavior. It simply means that you must treat them with the same love, respect, understanding, and forgiveness that you expect to receive when you fail.

"A soft answer turns away wrath." (Proverbs 15:1) A reverent fear of the Lord and a desire to live a life that is pleasing to God will help you to achieve this goal. Loving those who have hurt you purifies you. It frees you from the bondage of bitterness and sin. It is difficult for someone to continue being mean to you when you respond in love.

The Mirror
What issues in my family need to be resolved so that I can walk in the love that God's word requires?

Five Second Fix-it:
I recognize that by loving others I am confirming my love for you. I will honor my family above myself. Thank you for teaching me how to love others even when their actions
make it difficult for me to do so.
Romans 12:10

SATAN'S WORK

Anger

Adam lay with his wife Eve, and she became pregnant and gave birth to Cain. She said, "With the help of the LORD I have brought forth a man." Later she gave birth to his brother Abel. Now Abel kept flocks, and Cain worked the soil. In the course of time Cain brought some of the fruits of the soil as an offering to the LORD. But Abel brought fat portions from some of the firstborn of his flock. The LORD looked with favor on Abel and his offering, but on Cain and his offering he did not look with favor. So Cain was very angry, and his face was downcast. Then the LORD said to Cain, "Why are you angry? Why is your face downcast? If you do what is right, will you not be accepted? But if you do not do what is right, sin is crouching at your door; it desires to have you, but you must master it." Now Cain said to his brother Abel, "Let's go out to the field." And while they were in the field, Cain attacked his brother Abel and killed him.

Genesis 4:1-8

Your Family God's Way

Through this passage we learn many things about the sin of anger. We learn through the example set by Abel that obedience brings acceptance and blessings. Cain shows us just the opposite. Through Cain, we learn that anger is a sin and sin brings pain, death, and destruction. Cain's jealousy and anger led to pain in his life, the death of his brother, and destruction of his family. Even as

16

Jesus was being hanged on the cross, he prayed to the Father for forgiveness of his transgressors. Without forgiveness, anger and bitterness will become a stronghold that will bind you to the ways of Satan. It will hinder you ability to love and live.

Within blended families, many times the pain and disappointment of divorce and separation manifests as anger. Overcoming this evil spirit requires that you choose to live holy and righteous. Be slow to anger and abounding in love. Trust God's word and know that he forgives sin and rebellion but he will not leave the guilty unpunished. Avoid allowing your anger draw you into sin but be silent and wait on the Lord. (Psalm 4:4) This is God's way, the right way, and the only way to keep anger from destroying your family. Be imitators of God. (Ephesians 5:1) Pursue righteousness, faith, love and peace with a pure heart.

1 John 2:5-6 tells us that obedience to God's word is the proof that he lives in us. If Jesus lives in us then sin cannot. This same obedience will not allow you to become angered by the trials of life. Walking as Jesus did requires that anger be removed and replace with love and forgiveness. This is the greatest commandment. As you obey his word and follow his commands he will set you high above your circumstances. You will be freed from the pain of feeling left out or second best and will walk in a place of joy and peace.

God did not give you a spirit of timidity, but a spirit of power, of love, and of self-discipline. (2 Timothy 1:7) Make a choice to overcome your fears of failure with perseverance and determination. Choose your battles. Search for insight into what is important to the viability of your family and then work to achieve those goals. Focus on what is good and build on it. Make the effort to work within your and your new families strengths. Recognize that trials will come but don't give up. Take your cares to the Father and leave them there. No problem is too big for him. He will resolve your problems and all things will work for your ultimate good.

The Mirror
What things have I allowed to anger me and draw me into sin?

Five Second Fix-it:
I recognize that anger and wrath leads to evil. Thank you for keeping from sinning in my anger. Instead, I choose to search my heart and be silent. I will wait on your unfailing justice to give me peace.
Psalm 37:8

DESTRUCTIVE DECEIT

Deception

Now the serpent was more crafty than any of the wild animals the LORD God had made. He said to the woman, "Did God really say, 'You must not eat from any tree in the garden'?" The woman said to the serpent, "We may eat fruit from the trees in the garden, but God did say, 'You must not eat fruit from the tree that is in the middle of the garden, and you must not touch it, or you will die.' " "You will not surely die," the serpent said to the woman. "For God knows that when you eat of it your eyes will be opened, and you will be like God, knowing good and evil." When the woman saw that the fruit of the tree was good for food and pleasing to the eye, and also desirable for gaining wisdom, she took some and ate it. She also gave some to her husband, who was with her, and he ate it. Then the eyes of both of them were opened, and they realized they were naked; so they sewed fig leaves together and made coverings for themselves.

Genesis 3:1-7

Your Family God's Way

Dishonesty hinders justice and ignores righteousness. This passage reveals three very important lessons about the destruction of deception. First and foremost, Satan is a liar. His tactics will always lead to destruction. Second, deception draws you away from God and his ability to cover you in times of trouble. Last, deception divides and destroys families. Unresolved issues

19

from previous relationships can cause tension and strife. As families are destroyed and new ones form, the resulting emotions may be bitterness and unforgiveness. Those who feel that they have been harmed may resort to lies and deception as a tactic for hindering the progression of the new family.

In many cases, children find themselves pawns for carrying out this evil tactic. Children may be manipulated into believing that their new step-parent is evil or mean. Some children are made to believe that their biological parent will not love them the same once he or she remarries. Still others are tricked into believing that their new step-parent will not love them the way their biological parent does. Children may respond by choosing sides; whether it be the side of the one whom they believe loves them or simply avoiding the one whom they believe doesn't. This is often a coping mechanism that offers comfort and security to them. Regardless of its origin, deception leaves the new family divided. In this place of division, love is hindered, growth is stunted, and the fate is destruction.

Blending a family God's way requires open and honest communication. Current and past relationship issues and their impact on your current family situation need to be resolved. Be mindful of the impact of your words on the people around you and your situation. Discuss your expectations of one another both before and during the marriage. Allow unrestricted yet respectful discussions of important issues such as individual roles and family goals.

God promises to protect you from those who malign you. (Psalms 12:5) He commands you to love your enemies and pray for those who persecute you. If feel that you have been harmed by the lies of others, renounce Satan's power and stand faithfully on God's Word. Separate the sin from the sinner. Recognize that your struggle is not against flesh and blood, but against the rulers, against the authorities, against the powers of this dark world and against the spiritual forces of evil in the heavenly realms. (Ephesians 6:12) Evil must be fought in the spirit realm. Sin must be countered with Truth. Your weapon is forgiveness. Pray for the soul of your transgressor knowing that they are under the power of an evil being whose only goal is destruction. Ask God to reveal his Truth to them and to guard your heart from earthly pain with spiritual love, strength, and wisdom. He will, simply because you asked and have the faith to believe that it is done. Be vigilant. Satan is persistent. Each time you are confronted with lies, confess your forgiveness and resolve with the matter. Then walk in the unconditional, unwavering forgiveness that God has given to you.

If you are the one perpetrating the lies upon someone else, recognize gossiping, lying, backbiting, and bitterness as sin. Confess your sin and pray for deliverance from the evil that binds you. God promises that everyone who asks receives; he who seeks finds; and he who knocks, the door will be opened. (Matthew 7:8)

The Mirror
What lies are hindering my ability to love in the fullness of God? What is God's Truth?

Five Second Fix-it:
Thank you for revealing to me the lies that seek to destroy me and my family. I recognize these as sin and I know that I must confront sin. I rebuke Satan's attack on me and my family in Jesus Name.
1 Timothy 2:14

DARKNESS UNSPOKEN

Fear

After the people saw the miraculous sign that Jesus did, they began to say, "Surely this is the Prophet who is to come into the world." Jesus, knowing that they intended to come and take him king by force, withdrew again to a mountain by himself. When evening came, his disciples went down to the lake, where they got into a boat and set off across the lake for Capernaum. By now it was dark, and Jesus had not yet joined them. A strong wind was blowing and the waters grew rough. When they had rowed three or three and a half miles, they saw Jesus approaching the boat, walking on the water; and they were terrified. But he said to them, "It is I; don't be afraid." Then they were willing to take him into the boat, and immediately the boat reached the shore where they were heading.
John 6:14-21

Your Family God's Way

In this passage of scripture Jesus shows us many things about how God views fear. As Jesus walked on water in the midst of the storm, the disciples became afraid. This symbolizes the presence of God even in the midst of your storm. Jesus walking on water was something that the disciples were unable to comprehend due to their lack of faith. Walking on water is not his only miracle. God is great and limitless even in the presence of a lack of faith. Once you understand his greatness you gain access to his limitless abilities and you realize that there is nothing to difficult for God. Your family issues, whatever they may be, are no match for the amazing power of God.

In blended families, issues will arise. Many issues are directly related to the varied backgrounds of the parents and/or the children. Do not allow fear to hinder your ability to act on your own behalf and the behalf of your family. Fear is a sin. It paralyzes you. It leads to avoidance of the issues rather than a resolution. This will worsen your situation and can even lead to destruction of the family unit. Fear reveals your lack of faith, not only to God but to the Satan as well. It tells God that you do not trust him to fulfill his promises for your life and inhibits your ability to walk in the blessings of God. It tells Satan, that your life and the life of your family is available to him for his taking. Trust me. He will take whatever he needs to take to destroy your family.

Every issue that stands to hinder the progression of your family must be addressed. Keeping God first will help you to overcome your fear and to speak openly and honestly about your concerns. Nothing should be said out of anger or frustration but only out of love. Ask the Lord to guide you on what to say. In the face of fear and doubt he is your strong tower. He will strengthen you so that you face your fears and take authority over Satan through Jesus Christ. Satan is a defeated foe. In his defeat, fear is rebuked and strength is restored. As life's trials come your way, even if you do not understand how or why. Remember that with God, all things are possible. In the midst of your trials and the fear and doubt that may accompany them, know that as you allow God into your life and give him power over your situations, he will do miraculous things in your life. He will order your steps, your ways, and your words. Fear will be exchanged for the strength to overcome and the peace to endure whatever life brings your way. Allow him to get into the boat with you. There the comfort that he offered to the disciples is available to you, as well. In your times of fear and doubt, seek him. He will reveal himself to you and will comfort your fears. He will replace your doubt with the faith to believe for victory over whatever binds you. He will sail the sometimes rocky seas of life with you and guide you along your predestined path. You will reach the shore, safe and sound. On that shore rests the Spirit-led family that God desires.

The Mirror
What fears must I confront to claim the life that God has for me and my family?

Five Second Fix-it:
Lord, I feel like war is breaking out around me but I will not fear. I will find confidence in you. Thank you for answering my prayers and delivering me from all my fears. Thank your for helping me to face life with Godly perseverance and strength.
Psalm 27:3 & 34:4

SILENT THIEF

Grief

Then, at the evening sacrifice, I rose from my self-abasement, with my tunic and cloak torn, and fell on my knees with my hands spread out to the LORD my God and prayed: "O my God, I am too ashamed and disgraced to lift up my face to you, my God, because our sins are higher than our heads and our guilt has reached to the heavens. From the days of our forefathers until now, our guilt has been great. Because of our sins, we and our kings and our priests have been subjected to the sword and captivity, to pillage and humiliation at the hand of foreign kings, as it is today. "But now, for a brief moment, the LORD our God has been gracious in leaving us a remnant and giving us a firm place in his sanctuary, and so our God gives light to our eyes and a little relief in our bondage. Though we are slaves, our God has not deserted us in our bondage. He has shown us kindness in the sight of the kings of Persia: He has granted us new life to rebuild the house of our God and repair its ruins, and he has given us a wall of protection in Judah and Jerusalem.

Ezra 9:5-9

Your Family God's Way

In biblical times, grief was portrayed by the tearing of clothing. In this passage of scripture Ezra is grieving over the disobedience of God's people. He is appealing to God for forgiveness and restoration. It provides insight into the destruction of grief.

Also note God's answer to grief and emotional healing.

Blended families may experience grief related to loss of a parent, loss of a marital union, or changes to any aspect of the family that was comfortable or pleasant. Divorce or the death of a parent can precipitate this emotion. Grief is a prison that hinders our ability to serve God. Ezra speaks of it lending them to captivity, death, pillage, and humiliation. Grief does the same thing in our lives. It stunts our ability to love God, our family, and ourselves. Grief dims our ability to see God's path. It prevents us from being all that God has called us to be and do.

If your child is experiencing a drastic change in any area of their behavior, performance, or life; especially in the presence of a recent life change like divorce or remarriage, consider the presence of grief. Children often deal with feelings of grief differently. Some children become rebellious, rude, or angry. Others become introverted or isolated. They may no longer be interested in the things in which they used to enjoy. Drastic changes in the grades of school-age children can indicate the presence of grief or depression.

Regardless of whether this destructive emotion affects adults or children, open, honest communication, with God, your family, and other Christians is the key. Set aside private time daily where you can express you pain to God. He is there waiting to provide everything you need to heal. Pray for deliverance from the spirit of heaviness. Then believe for your healing and restoration. Don't let the enemy tell you anything different. Stand faithfully on God's word knowing that by his stripes you are healed. Speak openly with your family about areas that ignite your feelings of sadness and grief. Allow them the opportunity to correct any contributions that they might make to your emotional distress. Speaking to a Christian counselor or leader in a bible-believing church can also help to redirect your thoughts toward the things of God.

Blending a family, especially in the face of grief, may be difficult. But the joy of the Lord is your strength.(Nehemiah 8:10) This joy sustains you through your sadness and lifts you above your circumstances. God will free your heart to love again and not half-heartedly but completely. Fix your eyes on Jesus. He is the author and finisher of your faith. You are that temple whose ruins will be rebuilt. When you reach out to God in the presence of grief and depression he wraps you in his powerful yet loving arms. In this place there is the peace you need to endure a brief period of mourning. He will give light to yours eyes so that you can see past your circumstances to where he wants to take you. This place lies far beyond your current sadness and disappointment. You will endure your grief for a season but "joy comes in the morning". God will preserve you for his purpose. There is a wall of protection around you and relief from the grief that binds you. In this place of solace, like Ezra you will find kindness, love, and the strength to rebuild your life. In this restoration, you will be able to love yourself, your family, and those entrusted to you through marriage in the wholeness of God.

The Mirror
Is grief hindering my ability to love myself, my family, and those around me? What is causing the grief that binds me?

Five Second Fix-it:
Thank you for helping me to overcome my grief by filling me with hope, joy, and peace.

Thank you for your compassion and unfailing love that allows me to rejoice with a joy that no one can take away.

John 16:22

THE TENTH COMMANDMENT

Jealousy

After David had finished talking with Saul, Jonathan became one in spirit with David, and he loved him as himself. From that day Saul kept David with him and did not let him return to his father's house. And Jonathan made a covenant with David because he loved him as himself. Jonathan took off the robe he was wearing and gave it to David, along with his tunic, and even his sword, his bow and his belt. Whatever Saul sent him to do, David did it so successfully that Saul gave him a high rank in the army. This pleased all the people, and Saul's officers as well. When the men were returning home after David had killed the Philistine, the women came out from all the towns of Israel to meet King Saul with singing and dancing, with joyful songs and with tambourines and lutes. As they danced, they sang: "Saul has slain his thousands, and David his tens of thousands." Saul was very angry; this refrain galled him. "They have credited David with tens of thousands," he thought, "but me with only thousands. What more can he get but the kingdom?" And from that time on Saul kept a jealous eye on David. The next day an evil spirit from God came forcefully upon Saul. He was prophesying in his house, while David was playing the harp, as he usually did. Saul had a spear in his hand and he hurled it, saying to himself, "I'll pin David to the wall." But David eluded him twice.

1 Samuel 18:1-11

Your Family God's Way

This passage reveals jealousy's destructive consequences. As the people began to praise David for his valor, the word says that Saul became angered. His anger evoked jealousy. The word says that the next day an evil spirit from God came forcefully on Saul. This spirit of jealousy led Saul to attempt to harm and eventually try to kill David, someone he once loved and respected. Saul's jealousy fueled a hatred that would lead to demise of the relationship and ultimately Saul's destruction.

Jealousy occurs when one person feels that he or she has been wronged. This is especially true in blended families where lives have been altered by death or divorce and healing has not occurred. Jealousy, a tool of mass destruction, can have the same destructive outcome in your family as it did for Saul. It is an evil spirit that opens the door for sin and division. It evokes feelings of anger which can lead you to hurt the ones you love. Its only purpose is to deter and distract believers and destroying families. Jealously, if not resolved, can consume you and your family and bring strife, unforgiveness, pain, and death.

Jealously, like all other sin, must be countered with Truth. Your greatest weapon against the spirit of jealousy is unconditional and sincere love. Love offers freedom. It covers a multitude of sin. Love purifies your heart giving you peace even in the face of a jealous spouse, ex-spouse, or child. As you love one another, God will live in you and his love will complete you. In the presence of God and his precious light, the darkness of jealousy cannot exist.

In a blended family time, resources, and especially love must be dispersed evenly and fairly. Feelings of jealousy or covetousness must be countered with loving correction and immediate attempts to remedy the situation. Devote yourself to one another. By doing so, you will find that your desire to honor your family will become greater than your own feelings of pride and insecurity. Your actions of obedience will free you to love the ones who have hurt you. It will also spur others on toward love and good deeds. This is especially true when a child is the perpetrator. As they feel loved they will give love and feelings of jealously and insecurity will dwindle.

Remember that you may not have control over the actions of other adults. If the jealousy is perpetrated by an ex-spouse and the sin cannot be addressed in non-confrontational way, take your petition to God. Cover your family in prayer. Pray for the wisdom and insight necessary to do battle in the spirit realm. Ask the Lord to give you the ability to recognize Satan's attempts and to endure them with Godly perseverance. Victory is yours because the battle has already been won. He will honor your prayers. God's word promises you healing, abundant peace, and security. You will find that Satan's fiery darts will no longer pierce you and the pain and hurt of jealousy will be numbed or totally removed.

The Mirror

Is jealousy hindering my ability to love or be loved? What areas must I address in my prayers to prevent jealousy from destroying me or my family?

Five Second Fix-it:
Thank you for delivering me and my family from the jealousy that seeks to divide us. I recognize that jealousy brings disorder. I choose today to counter it with love, patience, and kindness. Thank you for showing me how.
1 Corinthians 13:4

THE MIRROR

Judgment

"Do not judge, or you too will be judged. For in the same way you judge others, you will be judged, and with the measure you use, it will be measured to you. "Why do you look at the speck of sawdust in your brother's eye and pay no attention to the plank in your own eye? How can you say to your brother, 'Let me take the speck out of your eye,' when all the time there is a plank in your own eye? You hypocrite, first take the plank out of your own eye, and then you will see clearly to remove the speck from your brother's eye.
Matthew 7:1-5

Your Family God's Way

Jesus taught that we should not be concerned about what others do or don't do. Instead, we should make sure that we are living a Christ-like life. In Matthew 7:1-5, Jesus shows how we often focus our attention on other peoples' faults while overlooking our own. He compares it to trying to get a speck of sawdust out of a friend's eye, while we have a huge stick in our own eye. Many people rationalized or excuse their own behavior. But God's word commands that we acknowledge our own problems and faults, before we try to correct the faults of others. This reference does not just apply to a neighbor or friend. It applies to our family as well. It is easy to find fault in an angry ex-spouse, a proud or jealous spouse, or a mean and selfish stepchild. But what about when you are acting the same way. Are you able to see your own

34

faults? When you do, are you willing and able to correct them? .

In James 1:23, Paul says that we have a mirror we can look into, the Holy Bible. The Bible tells us how we are to live by telling us how Jesus lived. It also helps us to measure the success of our attempts and describes for us the consequences and rewards our obedience. Then the choice is up to us. We have free will. The will to obey or disobey; to live or die. When trials come, chose life. Ask yourself, "What would Jesus do in this situation?". When you are tempted to speak in anger or frustration, ask "What would Jesus say?". When you struggle with wrong and right, ask, "What does the Bible say about ... ?". Remember that we all have to answer to God, not each other. Knowing this will keep you from falling into sin as a response to the actions of others.

Not judging does not mean that we do reveal to others when they are sinning. Jesus frequently taught people right from wrong, based on God's Word. But we should not consume ourselves with the faults of others so much so that we area blinded to our own problems. We should instead help others to overcome sin in their lives by setting a Godly example ourselves. When conflict arises, listen and affirm what is being said. Then speak only what is truthful and edifying to your spouse, your children, and even those who have harmed you. Help them return to righteousness in love.

Blending a family God's way demands that you not judge the actions of those around you. If hostility and hurt from past interactions are the source of your judgmental attitude, forgiveness is the answer. We are commanded to forgive those who have harmed us. You are commanded to love the children entrusted to you, whether biological or through marriage; good or bad. Avoid sinning in your words, thoughts, and actions. If your own insecurities are fueling your judgmentalism, ask God to help you to see yourself the way he sees you," fearfully and wonderfully made".

The Mirror
Is the reflection that I see in the mirror the image of Christ? If not, what areas in my life must I work on so that I can be secure and no longer feel the need to judge others?

Five Second Fix-it:
I will not judge others but instead show them how to live through my example. Thank you for showing me how to forgive so that I can be forgiven and how to love so that I can be loved.
Luke 6:37

INVISIBLE LOVE

Loneliness

Then Moses went out and spoke these words to all Israel: "I am now a hundred and twenty years old and I am no longer able to lead you. The LORD has said to me, 'You shall not cross the Jordan.' The LORD your God himself will cross over ahead of you. He will destroy these nations before you, and you will take possession of their land. Joshua also will cross over ahead of you, as the LORD said. And the LORD will do to them what he did to Sihon and Og, the kings of the Amorites, whom he destroyed along with their land. The LORD will deliver them to you, and you must do to them all that I have commanded you. Be strong and courageous. Do not be afraid or terrified because of them, for the LORD your God goes with you; he will never leave you nor forsake you." Then Moses summoned Joshua and said to him in the presence of all Israel, "Be strong and courageous, for you must go with this people into the land that the LORD swore to their forefathers to give them, and you must divide it among them as their inheritance. The LORD himself goes before you and will be with you; he will never leave you nor forsake you. Do not be afraid; do not be discouraged."
Deuteronomy 31:1-8

Your Family God's Way

Moses was old and no longer able to lead the Israelites. So the Lord makes a promise of fulfillment to comfort him and his followers. God promises to go into the land and destroy the

37

nations before them so that the Israelites could possess the Promised Land. He reassures them that they will never be alone. He will always be with them. His only requirement is that the Israelites follow his commands.

This passage of scripture provides a roadmap for overcoming the sin of loneliness. Loneliness is a lie from the pit of Hell. Satan uses it to isolate you from the unified battle team of your family and those around you who can intercede on your behalf. There in your isolation, you will be forced to fight alone. Warring against demonic forces can be a long, hard, and deadly battle. Without the intercessory strengths of your natural and Christian family, you may get weary and weary warriors face certain death.

Loneliness is not an uncommon emotion in blended families. Children often side with one parent or the other. They may feel isolated as a result of new rules or new living arrangements. Some children isolate themselves in response to feeling unwanted or left out. This emotion is not an emotion common only to the children of blended families. Parents may experience loneliness for many reasons. One common reason is that parents often choose biological children over step-children in response to guilt over the divorce or death of a spouse. Some parents side with the children over their mate. Many try to fill a perceived void or soothe feelings of a perceived loss. Parents also experience loneliness as a result of placing too much emphasis on the new family and not enough on the marital union.

Loneliness, although not uncommon, is ungodly. It is sin that must be countered with God's word. Do not believe the lies of the enemy. Avoid the temptation of isolation as a solace for feeling left out, alone, or unwanted. You are never alone. God is always with you. He will never leave you nor forsake you. Just as he did for Moses and the Israelites, he goes into battle ahead of you, fights with you, and intercedes on your behalf when you grow weary. His only requirement is that you follow his commands. The greatest of these commands is that you love your neighbor; your children and your mate; as yourself. (Mark 12:31)

Draw near to God in the midst of your loneliness. He will wrap you in the love necessary to draw your family closer together. This means putting away bruised egos, anger, fear, and doubt. It means stepping out on faith. Not every effort will be met with acceptance; but love conquers all. As you reach out to your new children in love and respect; they will reach out to you. Anger, disrespect, and rejection cannot exist in the presence of such love. Seek out opportunities to blend your family in the unconditional and unfailing love of God. Take time to get to know your children's likes and dislikes. Discover their needs and make meeting those needs a priority in your life. Set aside time alone with both your mate and your children. This not only ensures fairness but prevents loneliness from finding a place in your life and your family. Spend quality time talking, laughing, and loving and there will be no time left for Satan's evil schemes.

Many children of blended families experience loneliness as well. In their times of loneliness, they too can find solace in the comfort of God's loving arms. Teach your children how to get into the presence of God. Teach them how to pray and submit to the guidance of the Holy Spirit. There is no age limit on God's company. Instill in them that God is able to be in many places at the same time and is always available to them whenever they need him. They too, are never alone.

The Mirror
What things can I do to replace my feelings of loneliness with the love of my family?

Five Second Fix-it:
Thank you for your presence which comforts me in my time of loneliness. Your word promises that you are always in the company of the righteous. Therefore, I find comfort in your unfailing love. Thank you for giving me the strength to overcome loneliness by sharing this love with others.
Deuteronomy 31:6 & Psalm 14:5

A FOOL'S WAR

Strife

Now Sarai, Abram's wife, had borne him no children. But she had an Egyptian maidservant named Hagar; so she said to Abram, "The LORD has kept me from having children. Go, sleep with my maidservant; perhaps I can build a family through her." Abram agreed to what Sarai said. So after Abram had been living in Canaan ten years, Sarai his wife took her Egyptian maidservant Hagar and gave her to her husband to be his wife. He slept with Hagar, and she conceived. When she knew she was pregnant, she began to despise her mistress. Then Sarai said to Abram, "You are responsible for the wrong I am suffering. I put my servant in your arms, and now that she knows she is pregnant, she despises me. May the LORD judge between you and me."

Genesis 16:1-5

Your Family God's Way

Strife is the result of many factors. Abram's adultery and Sarai's lack of faith opened the door for a spirit of strife to operate in their household. Sarah felt that if she couldn't give Abraham a son, Hagar could. She failed to rely on God to give them both a son. Sarai's sin resulted in jealousy and anger and caused strife between her and Abram. This is the case in many families today. A lack of faith may result in frustration and disappointment. Operation outside of God's will puts the family at risk for demonic activity, division, and destruction. Strife is just one of Satan's many tactics.

Overcoming strife in any family situation but especially a blended family requires that strife be recognized as sin. It is one of Satan's many tactics of destruction. Strife must be rebuked. Rebuking strife requires that you remain committed to God in everything. This not only refers to finances but to your marriage, your children's upbringing, and yourself. Within that commitment, you and your family will be able to walk in the love, patience, and forgiveness that God's word calls for. Your family's success is dependent on you standing as a unified front against evil. Two of your greatest weapons against the spirit of strife are humility and forgiveness. Humility reveals your powerlessness without God and your strength with him. It causes you to seek insight from God regarding your actions and their affect on the lives of those around you. Forgiveness allows you to move past the offenses of others and your own indiscretions to a place of security, love, and the desire to resolve any conflict for the glory of God.

Never forget the power of the Holy Spirit to guide your ways, words, and actions for the preservation and promotion of your family. God's word will dictate the rules. Each parent must be empowered to communicate to the children their expectations of obedience. Unity preserves the peace of your family. When strife occurs among parents, they must make a choice to support each other in the presence of the children. Then take time to discuss and resolve the conflict later when the children are no longer present. When children see that both parents are in agreement they recognize their powerlessness to manipulate the strength of your unity. This will empower the children to remain unified and encourage compliance with the rules of the home. Refuse to allow strife among your children, as well. Encourage open, honest, yet respectful discussion of the issue. Parents are obligated to act as an impartial liaison and to work for quick and fair resolution. Where two or more are joined together in Jesus' name, there will he be also. As you and your family stand in agreement on the things of God, he will plant himself in the midst. He will order your steps and the steps of your family along the path that he has set before you.

In my family, my husband and I live by the "our child" motto. There is no "his child" or "my child". Our girls are "ours". We stand together, fight together, and love together.
Your family God's way means living by the "our child" model. It has a 100% success rate and rebukes strife because it is modeled after the unconditional, unyielding love of Christ. In this model, you and your spouse must take joint responsibility for the children entrusted to you. Remember that when one person tries to force his/her way in, the resulting emotions may be jealousy, rejection, anger, resentment, and resistance. In this situation, strife opens the door for more sin, death, and destruction. Get rid of the "your child" or "my child" mind-set. All rules are agreed upon by both parents. The responsibility of love and discipline is equally shared by both

parents. Instead of competing for time, each parent must encourage their spouse to be involved in all aspects of the children's rearing. Be unified in your sacrifices and your rewards. As the enemy comes to bring strife into your family, stand as a unified front against him. Like all challenges, this one offers unlimited rewards and overwhelming joy if you succeed and with God's word leading the way, success is imminent.

The Mirror
Am I living the life of humility and forgiveness that God's word calls for? If not, what can I do to remove this sin from my life so that I can live a strife-free life?

Five Second Fix-it:
I understand that anger and jealousy produces strife. Thank you for removing strife from my family by helping us to pursue your plans for our lives above anything else.
Proverbs 30:33

HIS STRIPES, YOUR HEALING

Healing

Then they cried to the LORD in their trouble, and he saved them from their distress. He brought them out of darkness and the deepest gloom and broke away their chains. Let them give thanks to the LORD for his unfailing love and his wonderful deeds for men, for he breaks down gates of bronze and cuts through bars of iron. Some became fools through their rebellious ways and suffered affliction because of their iniquities. They loathed all food and drew near the gates of death. Then they cried to the LORD in their trouble, and he saved them from their distress. He sent forth his word and healed them; he rescued them from the grave. Let them give thanks to the LORD for his unfailing love and his wonderful deeds for men.
Psalm 107:13-21

Your Family God's Way

Second marriages are usually the result of a traumatic ending. Some are the result of the death of a spouse. Others are the product of divorce and very few marriages end amiably in this situation. Regardless of the precipitating event, healing is necessary to the success of the new family. After death of a spouse or a marital union and even into the new marriage, kids and parents both struggle with a sense of loss or the perception of loss; This can lead to feelings of intense sadness, anger, self-pity, failure, and guilt. Blended families do not have the luxury of shared family histories, memories, or practices. This may result in loyalty conflicts for the children who may feel obligated to choose one side or the other. The grief associated with the loss coupled with confusion about new family roles may aggravate an already difficult situation. While many adults find themselves trying to understand what went wrong, children are often left to deal with their own feelings of guilt, pain, anger, and loneliness, alone.

The Lord heals the brokenhearted and binds up their wounds. (Psalm 147:3) Blending a family, God's way, demands that each person be completely healed from previous hurts. This healing can only be found in the presence of God. It is available to adults and children alike. Healing requires that you identify thoughts and actions that are contrary to God's word and make a conscious decision to change. Ask God for deliverance from whatever binds you. He will deliver you from the bondage of your pain and promote you to a place of forgiveness, joy, and peace. After you have suffered a little while, the God of all grace, who called you to his eternal glory in Christ, will himself restore you and make you strong, firm and steadfast. (1 Peter 5:10)

Do not let the trials of life hinder your love walk. God will strengthen you through your trials as you stay "fully committed to him". He will give you the endurance and encouragement you need to claim healing and restoration for your family. Children often need your help with this process. Encourage them to discuss their feelings openly and honestly. Reinforcing your love for them will give them the strength to overcome their pain and to grow into completely restored adults.

If you have tried everything you know and are still unable to overcome your sadness, pain, or depression, reevaluate the level of your faith. In the absence of the ability to believe for your healing and the preservation of your family; you may need someone to stand in agreement with you. You may need someone to pray and intercede on your behalf. Keep in mind that blending a family God's way requires that God remains first in your life. Seek guidance from a religious leader or any bible-believing Christian. Avoid seeking worldly help for a spiritual problem. Seek the Lord about whom you should consult then be obedient to his directions for your life and the lives of your family. Experts say, "Healing may take time"; some say as long as five years. But I say, just like the woman with the issue of blood, your healing can be instant and complete. You can be restored to wholeness and live to love again.

Everything you need lies in Jesus Christ. He is the answer. In times of depression and disappointment, the word of God serves as a tool of eternal solace and strength. Power lies in your commitment and obedience to God and his mandates for your life. This power fuels a desire to live out the perfect will of God. Press past your limitations and shortcomings. Do not be deterred. Everything that God says is yours is waiting for you. The joy, healing, and restoration you need is waiting to be claimed. Claim it.

The Mirror
What unresolved pain is hindering my ability to love wholly and unconditionally?

Five Second Fix-it:
Thank you for your sacrifice by which my healing was bought and for helping me to walk in the wholeness that is required to be a pillar of faith for myself and my family.
Isaiah 53:5

THE POISON

Forgiveness

Then Peter came to Jesus and asked, "Lord, how many times shall I forgive my brother when he sins against me? Up to seven times?" Jesus answered, "I tell you, not seven times, but seventy-seven times. "Therefore, the kingdom of heaven is like a king who wanted to settle accounts with his servants. As he began the settlement, a man who owed him ten thousand talents was brought to him. Since he was not able to pay, the master ordered that he and his wife and his children and all that he had be sold to repay the debt. "The servant fell on his knees before him. 'Be patient with me,' he begged, 'and I will pay back everything.' The servant's master took pity on him, canceled the debt and let him go. "But when that servant went out, he found one of his fellow servants who owed him a hundred denarii. He grabbed him and began to choke him. 'Pay back what you owe me!' he demanded." His fellow servant fell to his knees and begged him, 'Be patient with me, and I will pay you back. '"But he refused. Instead, he went off and had the man thrown into prison until he could pay the debt. When the other servants saw what had happened, they were greatly distressed and went and told their master everything that had happened. "Then the master called the servant in. 'You wicked servant,' he said, 'I canceled all that debt of yours because you begged me to. Shouldn't you have had mercy on your fellow servant just as I had on you?' In anger his master turned him over to the jailers to be tortured, until he should pay back all he owed. "This is how my heavenly Father will treat

each of you unless you forgive your brother from your heart."
Matthew 18:21-35

Your Family God's Way

The parable above is a very real and poignant demonstration of the importance of forgiveness. It incorporates three major themes. First, God's forgiveness is unconditional and requires only that we ask for it. Second, God expects us to forgive others in the same way that we expect him to forgive us. Last, disobedience to this command will render us prisoners of sin. It lends us to the torture and destruction of bitterness, condemnation, and revenge.

For the first servant, forgiveness from his master allowed him to free from bondage and to have all of his debts cancelled. This is very much so how the forgiveness of God is. It is a promise that is unconditional. All we have to do is ask in repentance and it is given, because God is faithful. The forgiven servant then goes out and attempts to collect a debt from another servant who owes him money. This is how many of us are when it comes to forgiveness. We don't want to forgive our brother or sister who has sinned against us but as soon as we fail, we expect God to forgive us. This parable offers a clear picture of the fate for these actions. Unforgiveness renders you a prisoner to the hope of revenge and the hopelessness of bitterness. It tortures you and prevents you from growing and progressing in the things of God.

In blended families, there may be many bruised egos and hurt feelings. Parents are adjusting to new children and a new spouse who may have different life experiences and expectations. Many parents are still trying to figure out just when things went wrong in their previous family. Children are often hurt by the changes to what they previously knew as their family. All of these situations can result in emotional responses that cause pain or anger in one family member or the other. But forgiveness is the key.

Moving past the guilt, pain, and hurt requires that there is total forgiveness, of God, yourself, and anyone that you feel has wronged you. Forgiveness is not always getting the response you want from others. Sometimes it is resolving the matter within yourself so that you can provide God-led correction to help the sinner return to righteousness. This may be unrealistic in situations where others are not accountable to the sovereign forgiving God we serve. Sometimes, forgiveness is simply resolving the issue within yourself. It is making a choice to walk in the love of God even in the face of evil. It is acknowledging that nothing you do is too appalling to be forgiven and that God expects the same level of forgiveness from you.

If you are dealing with guilt about the failure of a previous marriage or family, repent. Guilt and condemnation are of the Devil. Ask God to deliver you from this bondage. Your shortcomings are a minor infraction when placed against the forgiveness of God. God will remember your sins no more. Just as God has forgiven you, you need to forgive yourself. Remember this promise when the enemy comes to condemn you. And he will. He will tell you that your sins are too great to be forgiven or your sickness is too severe to be healed. This is a lie from the pit of Hell created by the author of lies, Satan. The blood of Jesus was poured out for your sins, your forgiveness, and your redemption..

If you are dealing with bitterness towards someone you believe has wronged you, Jesus offers one of the greatest examples of forgiveness you will ever see. He went through life here on earth being ridiculed, mistreated, beaten, and ultimately murdered. Yet, his last words, before the Father was a petition of forgiveness for his offenders. This is your life's challenge. Forgive as he forgave so that you can walk in the freedom and abundance that He offers.

The Mirror
Have I been holding myself hostage in my own mind by harboring unforgiveness in my heart? What can I do to resolve the issue?

Five Second Fix-it:
Thank you helping me forgive myself and those who have wronged me. I know that bitterness holds me captive and forgiveness frees me. I want to be free in

you. Thank you for helping me to remove malice from my heart so that I can walk in the love that you require.
Acts 8:23

BRAIN BRAWL

Attitudes and Actions

Do not be anxious about anything, but in everything, by prayer and petition, with thanksgiving, present your requests to God. And the peace of God, which transcends all understanding, will guard your hearts and your minds in Christ Jesus. Finally, brothers, whatever is true, whatever is noble, whatever is right, whatever is pure, whatever is lovely, whatever is admirable—if anything is excellent or praiseworthy—think about such things. Whatever you have learned or received or heard from me, or seen in me—put it into practice. And the God of peace will be with you.

Philippians 4:6-7

Your Family God's Way

Jesus taught that our words and actions are not the only parts of our beings that are regulated by God's Law. Our thoughts are to be controlled as well. Holding a grudge or wishing someone harm is just as bad, if not worse than causing them physical harm. This is because what we think commands what we do. If you allow it, your mind can make you a prisoner of sin. As you allow evil thoughts to enter your mind, your body will follow.

Blending a family God's way is all about attitudes. Matt 15:18-19 says that the things we speak come from the heart. If they are negative they can defile you. This verse goes on to say that out of the heart proceeds evil thoughts and avoiding evil demands that you control your thoughts. Search yourself to identify thoughts that are contrary to God's word. Then make a conscious choice to change your thinking for the glory of God and the preservation of your family. Anger must be countered with thoughts of calmness and love. Jealousy is countered with thanksgiving. Bitterness cannot exist in the presence of forgiveness. Sin is countered with obedience.

Blending your family God's way requires that you face life changes differently from the world. Anger, frustration, disappointment, and depression are not an option. Once you give your life to Christ, you must be transformed by the renewing of your mind. This transformation allows you to prove what God's will is through your obedience to his word. His will is good, pleasing, and perfect. Keeping your mind on Jesus will help you to endure the trials your new family will face with joy and perseverance. Renewing your mind allows you to face a disgruntled ex-spouse, an isolated child, or an angry step-child with godliness and righteousness. A renewed mind is clear-minded and self-controlled. It is able to develop new decision-making skills as a family unit in accordance to the word of God. Your renewed mind redefines your values for the growth and strength of your new family. It rejoices in the blessing of a new family and a fresh start.

Step-children may come to you battered, tattered, and broken. If you hide your knowledge, you become useless to them. This knowledge will reveal to you what they need to be restored. If you respond to their darkness with anger, frustration, and disappointment, they will be unable to see their way out of darkness. They will either become lost or find solace in the darkness.

A light shines in the darkness so that others can find their way. It helps people to see clearly the path set before them. Children of blended families need salt and light. They need Godly parents who add flavor to their lives. They expect their innocence to be preserved and this preservation only comes by edification. Focus on the positives. Try to precede constructive feedback with reinforcement of the positives. Be careful not to negate the negatives. Speak honestly and firmly about areas of change. Do not accept failure as an option for your children or your family. Avoid responding in anger. Anger dims your light by drawing you into the same darkness that you are responding to.

The path of your children must be lit with discipline, compassion, and love. Anyone can develop the Godly attitudes necessary to the preservation of their family. All you have to do is ask, believe, and act. Form the thought of commitment to obedience in your head and pray to God for victory in this area. Then believe that you are everything that God says you are and your family needs you to be. Walk in the godliness that you family expects and expect the same from those around you. Guard your thoughts and your actions by keeping your mind stayed on the things of God. Whatever is true, whatever is noble, whatever is right, whatever is pure, whatever is lovely, whatever is admirable—if anything is excellent or praiseworthy—think about such things. (Philippians 4:8) God will give you control over your words, thoughts, and actions. He will help you to walk in the fullness of his grace so that you can be all that he has called you to be. He will help you to be a blessing to those around you and to fill their voids for his glory.

The Mirror
What thoughts have I had that are contrary to God's Word and detrimental to my family's well-being?

Five Second Fix-it:
Thank you for renewing my mind. Thank you for transforming me into an image more like yours. I will keep my mind on you so that I can maintain perfect peace within your perfect will.
Romans 12:2

Controlling your tongue

Then some Pharisees and teachers of the law came to Jesus from Jerusalem and asked, Why do your disciples break the tradition of the elders? They don't wash their hands before they eat!" Jesus replied, "And why do you break the command of God for the sake of your tradition? For God said, 'Honor your father and mother' and 'Anyone who curses his father or mother must be put to death.' But you say that if a man says to his father or mother, 'Whatever help you might otherwise have received from me is a gift devoted to God,' he is not to 'honor his father' with it. Thus you nullify the word of God for the sake of your tradition. You hypocrites! Isaiah was right when he prophesied about you: " 'These people honor me with their lips, but their hearts are far from me. They worship me in vain; their teachings are but rules taught by men.'" Jesus called the crowd to him and said, "Listen and understand. What goes into a man's mouth does not make him 'unclean,' but what comes out of his mouth, that is what makes him 'unclean.' "
Matthew 15:1-10

Your Family God's Way

This scripture is very clear about how important controlling the things we say is to God.

There are two sides to this command. First, we must be cognizant of our behavior as it relates to the things we say. Hypocrisy, as Jesus calls it, is a sin. He refers to the hypocrisy of the Pharisees

58

with disgust. God wants our words to not only line up with his Word and his will but he demands that our actions do as well. Second, we must always be cognizant of the power of our words. With our words, we have the ability to impact not only our lives but the lives of the people around us. It is important to honor God by speaking only those things that glorify him and edify his people.

Many people who believe that they have been harmed by others may be tempted to respond with a verbal barrage of insults, lies, and slander. This is especially true in blended families where unresolved pain and unforgiveness may open the door of demonic activity. But this is not God's way. It is not his will for any person or any family.

The bible presents a very strong opinion of our tongue and its power to either give life or destroy life. James 3:6 says that the tongue sets the whole course of your life on fire and is itself set on fire by hell. God has given you power over hell and all of its destructive devices. Use it to claim the blessings of God for you and your family. James 3:2 goes on to say that if you control your tongue you can control your whole body. Our words control our actions. Gaining the ability to control what we say allows us to control the course of our life. Our words activate our faith and give us the power to speak good things into existence. Speak love over your children and your mate. Speak strength, wisdom, and protection over your life. Whatever you needs lies in your ability to claim it.

Proverbs 6:16-20 describes the seven things that the LORD finds detestable. They are haughty eyes, a lying tongue, hands that shed innocent blood, a heart that devises wicked schemes, feet that are quick to rush into evil, a false witness who pours out lies, and a man who stirs up dissension among brothers. Lies, slander, and deception can be appropriately placed in any of these categories. Is being detestable to God and option for you? If you are the perpetrator of such sin, confess it and make a conscious choice to change your behavior. Preserving you family demands that you choose to speak life into the people that God has entrusted to you; your family. Edify them when they are up, encourage them when they are down, lift them up when they fall, and stand in the gap when they can no longer stand for themselves. This is God's command for you.

If you are the person who has been harmed by such sin, recognize Satan's trap. He will try to entice you to sin as a response to your pain. Make a choice to respond to in loving, truthful, and God-led correction. This does not in any way imply that the negative behavior is ignored. It simply means that you fight spiritually and without God warriors become weary. The Word says that in the absence of God, the tongue becomes a restless evil full of deadly poison. This is especially true in situations where pain has been allowed to germinate until it is most potent. As with any poison, the more potent, the more deadly. This poison will not only destroy the spirit of the people around you, it will destroy you as well. Reclaiming your life means refusing to gossip, backbite, and speak in anger over those around you. Choose to edify instead of criticize. Ask the Holy Spirit to deliver you from the desire to respond carnally and to give you the strength to endure your trial with godly perseverance and righteousness. God will honor your obedience. He will bless you with a peace that surpasses all understanding and abundant joy. In this place of blessing, you will be healed from your hurt and freed to live and love again.

The Mirror
What things have I said to my family that dishonor God? What responses can I replace them with?

Five Second Fix-it:
I know that I have the power of life and death in my words. Today I choose life. I will speak only those things that glorify you. Thank you for giving me the words to say to be a blessing to my family and to enrich my life.
Proverbs 18:21

IN DUE SEASON

Patience

When the people saw that Moses was so long in coming down from the mountain, they gathered around Aaron and said, "Come, make us gods who will go before us. As for this fellow Moses who brought us up out of Egypt, we don't know what has happened to him." Aaron answered them, "Take off the gold earrings that your wives, your sons and your daughters are wearing, and bring them to me." So all the people took off their earrings and brought them to Aaron. He took what they handed him and made it into an idol cast in the shape of a calf, fashioning it with a tool. Then they said, "These are your gods, O Israel, who brought you up out of Egypt." When Aaron saw this, he built an altar in front of the calf and announced, "Tomorrow there will be a festival to the LORD." 6 So the next day the people rose early and sacrificed burnt offerings and presented fellowship offerings. Afterward they sat down to eat and drink and got up to indulge in revelry. Then the LORD said to Moses, "Go down, because your people, whom you brought up out of Egypt, have become corrupt. They have been quick to turn away from what I commanded them and have made themselves an idol cast in the shape of a calf. They have bowed down to it and sacrificed to it and have said, 'These are your gods, O Israel, who brought you up out of Egypt.' "I have seen these people," the LORD said to Moses, "and they are a stiff-necked people. Now leave me alone so that my anger may burn against them and that I may destroy them. Then I will make you into a great nation."
Exodus 32:1-10

Your Family God's Way

In the midst of anger, strife, and pain; one day can seem like years. Many people respond to these emotions with a haste to put an end to the behavior igniting the conflict. But how long is long enough? Only God knows. "Be still before the Lord and wait patiently for him; do not fret when men succeed in their ways, when they carry out their wicked schemes. (Psalms 37:7) God will strengthen you with all power according to his glorious might. Though this power you will gain endurance and patience for the task at hand.

There is a time for everything, and a season for every activity under heaven:
Ecclesiastes 3:1 When it comes to blended families, many people expect that after the wedding, everything will be smooth sailing. This is very seldom the case. There will be many obstacles to overcome. But all offer victory if you allow God to guide the ship. He has a pre-destined path for your life and the lives of your family. Along this path are many twists and turns and maybe even some rough seas. But just like he did for the disciples, he will calm the seas and deliver you to a victorious place of unity and wholeness.

In times of trouble, remain joyful in hope, patient in affliction, and faithful in prayer. (Romans 12:12) God will resolve the conflict in your life and bring you to a place of peace and joy. As you wait patiently on Him, even when there is tension and strife you will find that you are able to exist in a place of joy and the hope of resolution through Jesus Christ. 1 Thessalonians 5:14 says that you must remain patient with everyone. Patience is the result of wisdom. It glorifies God to overlook the offenses of others and to wait on the Lord for resolution. His word promises that those who have the faith and patience will inherit what has been promised. God will do what His word says he will do. He will honor your obedience and diligence to serve him. He will bless you and your family with the desires of your heart. That loving relationship with your step-children, your children, and your spouse will be yours.

The Mirror
What needs have I been impatient with God about? Do I not trust his Word that he is faithful in *everything?*

Five Second Fix-it:
Thank you for giving me the strength and endurance to face the tasks at hand. I trust you to meet all of my needs in due season. I will remain joyful in hope, patient in affliction, and faithful in prayer.
Romans 12:12

THE POTTER'S HOUSE

Respect

Then David and all the men with him took hold of their clothes and tore them. They mourned and wept and fasted till evening for Saul and his son Jonathan, and for the army of the LORD and the house of Israel, because they had fallen by the sword. David said to the young man who brought him the report, "Where are you from?" "I am the son of an alien, an Amalekite," he answered. David asked him, "Why were you not afraid to lift your hand to destroy the Lord's anointed?" Then David called one of his men and said, "Go, strike him down!" So he struck him down, and he died. For David had said to him, "Your blood be on your own head. Your own mouth testified against you when you said, 'I killed the Lord's anointed.'"

2 Samuel 1:11-16

Your Family God's Way

God's stance on the respect of others is very clear. His word demands that we show proper respect to everyone.(1 Peter 2:17) Respect is God-ordained and mandated in his word. The above scripture reference demonstrates David's dedication to his leader despite Saul's demeaning and hurtful behavior. Blended families bring many different morals, values, and belief systems into one unit. In this situation, mutual respect is an essential component to avoiding the problems that can sometimes arise. God-led parenting is essential in the survival of a blended family. Understanding and/or respect for each other's basic values and priorities is essential to its success. Expectations of respect must be based on the word of God and nurture obedience. There must be mutual agreement and enforcement by both parents within the new family. Include consequences for disobedience and rewards for obedience.

Only be careful, and watch yourselves closely so that you do not forget the things your eyes have seen or let the slip from your heart as long as you live. Teach them to your children and to their children after them. (Deuteronomy 4:9) Parents must maintain a life that can be respected by their children. Parents are to set an example through their words and actions. The "Do as I say, not as I do" philosophy is not acceptable in God's eyes. The righteous man leads a blameless life; blessed are his children after him. (Proverbs 20:7) Parents must remember that they are clay in the hands of the great potter, the Heavenly Father. Just as God molds the parents into his glorious image, parents are charged with the responsibility of molding the children entrusted to them, as well. They must also be cognizant of their role as a parent and the obligation to meet the physical, emotional, and spiritual needs of the children.

The issue of respect cannot be discussed without addressing the area of discipline. Blended families may experience more difficulty in this area due to different parenting styles and levels of correction. Blending a family God's way demands that each person respect the other's parenting style and that parents provide instruction in the best interest of the child. Discipline must be carefully but firmly enforced with patience and love. Equally important to the survival of the family is that children understand the importance of respect for authority. With this moral kept in the forefront the temptation to disrespect any adult, whether biological or step-parent, will not be an option.

The Mirror
Am I setting a Christ-led example for my family? If not, what areas of deliverance must I pray for?

Five Second Fix-it:
I understand that respect for your commands offers a reward. Thank you for helping me to live a life that is pleasing to you so that I can be a Godly example for my children and my mate.
Deuteronomy 4:9

THE ROOT OF ALL EVIL

Stewardship

Jesus told his disciples: "There was a rich man whose manager was accused of wasting his possessions. So he called him in and asked him, 'What is this I hear about you? Give an account of your management, because you cannot be manager any longer.' "The manager said to himself, 'What shall I do now? My master is taking away my job. I'm not strong enough to dig, and I'm ashamed to beg— I know what I'll do so that, when I lose my job here, people will welcome me into their houses.' "So he called in each one of his master's debtors. He asked the first, 'How much do you owe my master?' " 'Eight hundred gallons of olive oil,' he replied. "The manager told him, 'Take your bill, sit down quickly, and make it four hundred.' "Then he asked the second, 'And how much do you owe?' " 'A thousand bushels of wheat,' he replied. "He told him, 'Take your bill and make it eight hundred.' "The master commended the dishonest manager because he had acted shrewdly. For the people of this world are more shrewd in dealing with their own kind than are the people of the light. I tell you, use worldly wealth to gain friends for yourselves, so that when it is gone, you will be welcomed into eternal dwellings. "Whoever can be trusted with very little can also be trusted with much, and whoever is dishonest with very little will also be dishonest with much. So if you have not been trustworthy in handling worldly wealth, who will trust you with true riches? And if you have not been trustworthy with someone else's property, who will give you property of your own? "No servant can serve two masters. Either he will hate the one and love the

other, or he will be devoted to the one and despise the other. You cannot serve both God and Money."
Luke 16:1-13

Your Family God's Way
The rich man and his dishonest manager reveal many things about the importance of stewardship. Their story explains the rewards of dealing fairly with others and especially in our finances. Just like the dishonest manager, God will demand that we give an account of all of the things entrusted to us. This includes our mate, our children, and our money. If we find ourselves unable to give a just, honest, and respectable account, we will be denied the Godly promotion necessary for spiritual growth, protecting our family, and fulfilling our destiny. We become spiritually stagnant. In the case of repeated abuse of the things entrusted to us, God may even demote us.

God's word offers a template for avoiding this place of destruction. You must prove your ability to be trusted with the small things so that God will bless you in abundance. In your obedience, he will make you a ruler over many things. Be trustworthy even when dealing with someone else's property. Loving and raising your step-children in the ways of the Lord ensures God that you will maintain the same kind of godliness and righteousness with your own children. Your efforts will be rewarded. Your family will be preserved and grow in the limitless possibilities of the kingdom of God.

This brings us to finances. Family finances can be a source of tension and strife, especially in blended families. Ex-spouses may be ordered to pay alimony of child support. When the ex remarries, his previous financial obligations do not stop. This means that money will be taken from the current family to pay for previous financial obligations. This often results in feelings of anger and frustration and even financial difficulty.

Unresolved debts can also be a source of strife in blended families. Success of the new family demands that both parents are in agreement when it comes to finances. There must be unity in deciding how all monies will be spent. The optimal plan would be for each party to resolve their own debts prior to marriage. For many this is unrealistic. If this is your situation, then you and your spouse must work together toward achieving your financial goals. Develop both short term and long terms goals for achieving financial stability. Keep your eye on the prize.

We must be good stewards over our finances. God promises to reward obedience in this area with prosperity and peace. Leviticus 19:13 tells us not to defraud our neighbor and to pay what is owed. As believers we must pay any monies that are due. This does not just include day to day expenses but any debt owed. If we do not pay our bills then we are guilty of sin.(Deuteronomy 24:15) If you owe alimony or child support, pay what is owed. If you have other debts, pay them. It is as simple at that. Not doing so is theft and theft is a sin. The wage of sin is death; death of a person, a union, or a family.

If you are on the receiving end of a financial blessing, use it for the purpose for which it was given. First, you must tithe. The tithe is a requirement of God's Law and it comes with a reward. Malachi 3:10 says "Bring the whole tithe into the storehouse, that there may be food in my house. Test me in this," says the LORD Almighty, "and see if I will not throw open the floodgates of heaven and pour out so much blessing that you will not have room enough for it." God will honor your obedience. You will find that you have more money than month. You will be blessed both financially as well as with peace of mind. God's floodgates will make sure that your ends not only meet but that they wrap around and around until you have the desires of you heart.

This brings us to the mommy-daddy factor with regard to finances. Ephesians 6:4 explains this very clearly. It states, "Fathers, do not exasperate your children; instead, bring them up in the training and instruction of the Lord. Children must be taught how to treat others, their belongings, and their finances. Teach them how to be good stewards by being good stewards yourself.

Tithing should be taught as soon as the children gain access to money, i.e. allowance, work, etc. To help my daughters learn this life-changing concept, I created a "money for God" jar. I decorated it in leopard print fur and pink ribbons. This made it attractive to them. It became fun to "save money for God". Encouraging tithing at an early age instills it into children before their tithe grows to an amount that will be attractive to keep.

Children must be taught the importance of helping others. Matthew 6:3 says that when we give to the needy that we not let our left hand know what our right hand is doing. He desires that our giving is done in secret, without pride, arrogance, or selfishness. God promises to reward this secret giving. Children must be taught the importance of giving unselfishly. One way to do this is to have periodic purge times. During these family events we encourage our daughters to go through their belongings and set aside any thing that they can no longer wear or no longer want. We package up every thing and donate it to our favorite charity. We make it a point to do this at least twice a year. Allow your children to make the decision to give cheerfully.   God   love   a   cheerful   giver. (2 Corinthians 9:7)

The Mirror
In what areas of stewardship do I need growth? What things must I change to be a good example to my children?

Five Second Fix-it:
Lord, I love you and I want to show my love by obeying your commands. Thank you for helping me to be a good example to my children by showing me how to be a cheerful and faithful tither. Thank you for meeting all

of my needs so that I can serve your people that they might see your glory.
2 Corinthians 9:7

Battle Gear For Weary Warriors

PETITIONS & PARDONS

Prayer
But when you pray, go into your room, close the door and pray to your Father, who is unseen. Then your Father, who sees what is done in secret, will reward you. And when you pray, do not keep on babbling like pagans, for they think they will be heard because of their many words. Do not be like them, for your Father knows what you need before you ask him.
Matthew 6:6-8

Your Family God's Way

The children of Israel are a great example of weary warriors. Wandering in the wilderness for forty years would probably make anyone weary. But the Israelites played a major part in the successes and failures of their journey. Their lengthy trial was the result of their disobedience. Their somnolence was the result of ungratefulness, unforgiveness, and their lack of faith. They often missed God's remedy to their problems because they were so caught up in the problem, itself. For most, failure and defeat was their fate.

Many Christians grow weary when their trials are challenging or prolonged. This is especially true when you have been worn down by the trials of life; anger, strife, and unresolved pain. If this is the case for you or your family members then consider the role of Moses. Like Moses, you may be the one chosen to speak on the behalf of your family. This role of intercessor can be filled by any bible-believing Christian, even your children. If you are the chosen one, it is essential that you know how to pray. It is equally important that your spouse and your children understand the importance of this powerful weapon and their authority through Jesus Christ. Matthew 21:22 says that "If you believe, you will receive whatever you ask for in prayer." Ask, believe and receive whatever you need for your burdens to be lifted and your family restored.

The prayer of a righteous man is powerful and effective. (James 5:16) Prayer is battle gear for weary warriors. It rejuvenates you and strengthens you for the battle at hand. Prayer gives you insight into God's plan for your life and the lives of your family members. It offers hope even in the dreariest of circumstances. Prayer builds faith so that you can see those things that are not as though they are. Prayer takes your heavy burdens to God. This brings a peace that surpasses all understanding. Prayer offers forgiveness, healing, joy, and restoration. It offers whatever you need to help your family to heal and to be restored.

So, how do you pray? You talk to God like the loving and forgiving God he is. He wants to be involved in your life and to be close to you. He is always willing and ready to talk but it up to us to approach Him. So how do you get God to hear you? Jesus is the way and the truth and the life. No one comes to the Father except through him. (John 14:6) Offer your prayers in Jesus' name. When you pray, Jesus intercedes on your behalf.

As he goes before the Father, God does not see you in your sin, he sees his blameless and righteous son before him. Through his love for the son who lives in you, he will honor your prayers.

Pray without ceasing. (1 Thessalonians 5:17) This does not mean habitual or thoughtless prayer. It means to honor God in everything. Acknowledge his greatness and faithfulness to fulfill *all* of his promises. Pray with a thankful heart and clean hands. This does not imply that you cannot come to God in your sin. It means that you bring your prayers of repentance to God to be redeemed. He will cleanse you of all unrighteousness. It also means making every effort to live in obedience, every day and in every way. Your thankfulness shows God how much you love him and clean hands allow you to receive his reciprocal love and abundant blessings.

Matthew 6:6 provides a wonderful template for prayer. It says, "When you pray, go into your room, close the door and pray to your Father, who is unseen. Then your Father, who sees what is done in secret, will reward you." Find your secret place where only you and God exist. Remove the distractions of the world. Pray to your heavenly Father who longs to shower you with his love. When God sees what is done in secret, he will reward you. Believe for your reward. It was claimed on Calvary with the blood of Jesus. It covers you and all that you hold near and dear. Your problems, circumstances, and trials become minor or non-existent in the presence of your powerful and efficient prayer.

IN ALL THINGS

Praise

After they had been severely flogged, they were thrown into prison, and the jailer was commanded to guard them carefully. Upon receiving such orders, he put them in the inner cell and fastened their feet in the stocks. About midnight Paul and Silas were praying and singing hymns to God, and the other prisoners were listening to them. Suddenly there was such a violent earthquake that the foundations of the prison were shaken. At once all the prison doors flew open, and everybody's chains came loose. The jailer woke up, and when he saw the prison doors open, he drew his sword and was about to kill himself because he thought the prisoners had escaped. But Paul shouted, "Don't harm yourself! We are all here!" The jailer called for lights, rushed in and fell trembling before Paul and Silas. He then brought them out and asked, "Sirs, what must I do to be saved?" They replied, "Believe in the Lord Jesus, and you will be saved—you and your household." Then they spoke the word of the Lord to him and to all the others in his house. At that hour of the night the jailer took them and washed their wounds; then immediately he and all his family were baptized. The jailer brought them into his house and set a meal before them; he was filled with joy because he had come to believe in God— he and his whole family.
Acts 16:23-34

Your Family God's Way

But in your hearts set apart Christ as Lord. Always be prepared to give an answer to everyone who asks you to give the reason for the hope that you have. But do this with gentleness and respect. 1 Peter 3:15 says "The Lord in His glory gives us so many reasons to praise Him." Look at your life. Has God not fulfilled all of his promises in your life? Has he not delivered you from the grasp of the enemy time and time again? Has there been even one of your needs that went unmet? I can say with 100% assurance, "No"!

Our victories through Him build faith in us. Praise serves as a testimony to others and reminds us of God's faithfulness. It manifests God's glory and magnifies His power to those who may not know Him. This is especially true in blended families where strife and tension has resulted in division. Praise will enable you to see past your current situation to the unity, joy, and love that God's word promises. It reminds us and shows others who may be lacking in faith that God is faithful.

Psalms 33:4 tells us that the word of the Lord is right, true, and that He is faithful in all he does. Praise is seeing things that are not as though they are. Praise tells others that God still performs miracles. We praise God in faith and when our praise brings forth a harvest, others are able to see God's glory. Luke 2:20 says that He is not a man that He should lie. He will do what He says He will do. Knowing this, we praise Him for what we know is already done to show others what God can do. This is especially true in the lives of our children who will face many things as they grow into productive, God-fearing adults. The power of praise will be an undeniable asset as they face the trials of puberty, peer pressure, and prejudice. It will help them to overcome these trials and temptations and to claim the victorious life God's word promises.

Praise God because His word demands it. Psalm 150:6 says, "Let everything that has breath praise the Lord". As believers we must be obedient to God's word in all aspects of our life and especially in the area of praise. Not doing so is sin and the wages of sin is death. God not only deserves your praise, he demands it. It's your choice, praise God because He deserves it or risk death; death of a person, a union, or a family.

Still not convinced? The bible always provides undisputable evidence. In Acts 16:23-26. Paul and Silas were unjustly cast into prison. They were severely beaten and fastened in stocks that bound their hands and feet in an immoveable position. The prison of that time was dark, damp, and stench-ridden with no bathroom facilities. But despite their circumstances, at midnight, they began to sing praises to the Lord. The joy of the lord was their strength. They were able to look past the outward to the eternal. They were able to see the unseen. Their joy brought the peace of God. Their praise propelled them into God's presence, provided a channel for God's power to operate in their circumstances, and allowed His power to operate for their release from bondage. The Word says that during their praying and singing, there was an earthquake that shook the prison. It shook so hard that the chains that bonded Paul, Silas, and <u>all</u> of the other prisoners were released. Do you have any chains in your life that need to be broken? Is tension and strife destroying your peace? Your family? Just like Paul and Silas, praise is the battle gear that will give you victory.

Even in the midst of the many trials you will face as your family is blended, praise can elevate you. It will lift you above your troubles to a place where you can see your blessings. It helps you to endure each trial knowing that trials work patience and through it you will be refined. You will come out better and stronger. I remember being in church many Sundays after being beaten up by an abusive spouse the night before. Praise lifted me above my circumstances. It brought me into a place of peace and joy. I was able to cry tears of joy even in my sorrow. I was able to shout God's praises even when the enemy, Satan, was trying to strangle me. I was able to rejoice even in my pain. Through my praise I was able to gain victory over my situation and come through the valley of the shadow of death unharmed. So can you.

MORE THAN NECESSARY FOOD

Fasting

"Is not this the kind of fasting I have chosen: to loose the chains of injustice and untie the cords of the yoke, to set the oppressed free and break every yoke? Is it not to share your food with the hungry and to provide the poor wanderer with shelter— when you see the naked, to clothe him, and not to turn away from your own flesh and blood? Then your light will break forth like the dawn, and your healing will quickly appear; then your righteousness will go before you, and the glory of the LORD will be your rear guard. Then you will call, and the LORD will answer; you will cry for help, and he will say: Here am I. "If you do away with the yoke of oppression, with the pointing finger and malicious talk, and if you spend yourselves in behalf of the hungry and satisfy the needs of the oppressed, then your light will rise in the darkness, and your night will become like the noonday.
Isaiah 58:6-10

Your Family God's Way

Fasting is abstaining from food for a spiritual reason. It is a spiritual affliction of the body. It is denying our flesh to allow spiritual breakthroughs to occur. It has been used for hundreds of years and for many different breakthroughs. Daniel, Moses, David, Nehemiah, Esther, and Jesus among many other people and groups, all fasted. It allows for clear communication with the Father and strengthens our relationship with Him. Fasting always occurs together with prayer. It adds power

83

to your prayers. You can pray without fasting but you can't fast without prayer.

Fasting serves many purposes. It is used to petition the Lord on your behalf or on behalf of someone else i.e. your spouse or your children. Fasting provides healing from emotional and physical pain. It is a form of praise to God. Fasting to incite humility. This is beneficial in removing jealousy, pride, and judgementalism from your family. Fasting is a tremendous weapon during spiritual warfare and provides supernatural provision for your needs. It can offer deliverance from bad habits, pain, and depression. Fasting increases your spiritual perception by removing distractions from your life to make God's revelations clear. So, when your trials seem bigger than you- Fast. God will welcome you into his presence. The enemy's distractions will be removed. You family will be everything you want it to be. More importantly, it will be everything God wants it to be.

FASTING CREED

Father God,

I am fasting for
(reason/s)_____
_____.

I will abstain from (food/meal)_____
for (time)_____.

I will focus my bible study on
(scripture/topics)_____
_____.

In Jesus' Name, Amen

Additional Titles by Dr. Sullivan:

- God's Money Your Wealth: Recession-Proofing Your Life God's Way
- The "I AM" Monologues: Sacred Sex in the Age of Perversion
- From Desperation to Destiny
- Toolkit for Broken People: Survival Guide for Victims of Abuse
- Mommy-Daddy Factor: Blending Your Family God's Way
- The Diamond Remedy: Hand-crafted By God For Marital Success
- Recovery: More Than One Day At A Time
- The Eleventh Commandment:
- Christ in the Workplace: The Employee Handbook

www.ingramcontent.com/pod-product-compliance
Lightning Source LLC
Chambersburg PA
CBHW060138050426
42448CB00010B/2193